Speaking Destruction Unto
DARK
RIVERS

Dr. D. K. Olukoya

Speaking Destruction Unto The Dark Rivers

DR. D. K. OLUKOYA

(2) Dr. D. K. OLUKOYA

SPEAKING DESTRUCTION UNTO THE DARK RIVERS
© 2009 DR. D. K. OLUKOYA
ISBN **978-0692260258**
October 2009

Published by:
Mountain of Fire and Miracles Ministries Press
13, Olasimbo Street, Onike, Yaba, Lagos.

All Scripture quotation is from the King James Version of the Bible

TABLE OF CONTENTS

.

CHAPTER ONE

SPEAKING DESTRUCTION UNTO THE DARK RIVERS

Jesus called the devil a liar and the father of all lies. Satan lies about everything. He wants to convince you that your problem has no solution. If you don't remember to stand by the word of God that nothing is impossible with Him, the devil will sweep you off your conviction and you will lose your expectation from the Lord.

John 8:44: Ye are of your father the devil, and the lusts of your father ye will do. He was a murderer from the beginning, and abode not in the truth, because there is no truth in him. When he speaketh a lie, he speaketh of his own: for he is a liar, and the father of it.

Satan knows the power of truth. Nothing in heaven and on earth can resist the power of the truth. Demons cannot withstand the power of the truth. What satan and demons do is to convince men to reject the truth and accept their errors and lies. Defeat is expressly certain when a believer shifts position from holding the truth to accepting falsehood.

Frustration and loss of hope are the consequences

of accepting the lies of the devil. Know it deeply in your heart that whatever the devil and demons tell you is nothing but a lie. The truth of the word of God has the power to convert, to save, to deliver and to heal. The devil knows it very well. He does not want you to continue in victory and in truth. He, therefore, sponsors lies and errors in order to cause a derailment. Don't yield to the lies of satan about your situation; your case is not beyond the power of God.

Mark 10:27: And Jesus looking upon them saith, With men it is impossible, but not with God: for with God all things are possible.

The word of God is resolute on the fact that all problems have solutions in God. There has never been a problem that God has had to refer to another source for solution. If God cannot solve a problem, who else can? Among men, problems are referred from one place to another, from one solution centre to another and from one approach to another. But God does not refer any problem to anybody. He does not reject any problem either. In heaven and on earth, all problems are referred to God who alone can solve them. Praise God!

Let me encourage you briefly before I proceed further. I want you to be certain that your problem has a solution with God. The woman with the issue of blood for 12 years had a strange and peculiar problem that defied all known solutions. When she got to Jesus, she received a solution to it. Lazarus was dead for four days and was already stinking in the grave. Mary and Martha, his sisters, were thrown into the problem of bereavement that could not be redeemed. Jesus arrived at the scene and all tears of sorrow were wiped away. It does not matter the name, the nature and the length of your problem, Jesus has all the solutions in His hands. He says, "Come!"

Matt. 11:28: Come unto me, all ye that labour and are heavy laden, and I will give you rest.

The devil has many weaknesses you need to know about. There are loopholes in his strategies because of his weaknesses and limitations. For instance, if satan knew his coup against God was going to fail, he would not have staged it. If he knew that the death of Jesus Christ would provide salvation for mankind, he would have let Him live forever. If the devil knew that attacking Job would result in his having twice as much as he ever had in all areas of his life, he would have let him remain as he was. The number one weakness of the devil is that he does not know everything and his limited knowledge creates loopholes in his strategies.

Another thing about the devil is that he is not present everywhere at the same time. He relies on the network of demons under his command. This is another weakness and limitation of his. If the demon he assigns to give him a report about somebody is arrested, the information cannot pass on to him. The moment a wicked power of darkness is intercepted through the prayer of a believer, it cannot fulfill the mission of the devil.

Prayer: Every messenger of the devil on assignment against me, fall down and die, in Jesus' name.

The third point about the devil is that his power is greatly limited. Jesus told the parable of an armed strongman, who kept his goods to illustrate satanic and demonic activities. The beautiful point in the parable is that it is possible for the strongman to be defeated by one stronger than he. The devil knows there is someone stronger than he. He knows there is someone who has all power, knowledge and wisdom at His disposal. His name is Jesus! Each time you shout that name loud in prayer, you fire an arrow at the forces of darkness.

Colossians 2:10: And ye are complete in him, which is the head of all principality and power.

The devil tries to conceal his weaknesses from you. Until you resist him according to the Scriptures, you will not know he will flee. Until you shout orders at him in the name of Jesus, you will not know that he and his demons can be subject to you.

Every Goliath has an unprotected forehead, which is a point of weakness. The fiery stones of prayer can penetrate his forehead and cause him to fall down and die. In the trial of Job, God gave the devil a limit he could go. Satan dared not go beyond that limit. The devil can be put under restriction by the power of God.

Job 1:12: And the Lord said unto Satan, Behold, all that he hath is in thy power; only upon himself put not forth thine hand. So Satan went forth from the presence of the Lord.

Problems are lies. The devil will make you to sit down and lament of a closed door. He will magnify to you what you would have gained if the door had not been closed. He would make sure you do not see the seven new doors that God wants to open in place of the closed one. The devil makes people to look at the size of their mountain. He blinds them to the power of God that had been there before any mountain was brought forth. Anything the devil does not want you to see is something meant to bring a turning point in your life.

Satan does not show anybody the real thing. He is just a liar and a deceiver.

During the temptation of Jesus Christ, the devil showed Him the kingdoms of the world and their glory. He promised to give them to Jesus if He would fall down and worship him. Jesus immediately knew his tricks and rebuked him.

Matthew 4:10: Then saith Jesus unto him, Get thee hence, Satan: for it is written, Thou shalt worship the Lord thy God, and him only shalt thou serve.

He showed Jesus the glory of the kingdoms of this world, but did not show Him the fire that will come and consume the kingdoms. He promised Jesus the kingdoms without revealing how the power of God would shake the world and no stone of any size would be left upon another. He showed Him the crown of the worldly kingdom, to divert Him from His focus on the incorruptible crown that will last for ever. The devil is a liar.

There is no truth in what satan shows you. He is trying to dazzle and deceive you with short-term glory, honour, fame, pleasure and wealth so that he can damn your soul eternally. The devil talks only about the pleasure of sin but never lets men see its consequences. He preaches repentance and forgiveness when trying to convince a believer to sin but never talks about the judgment and the losses the sinner will suffer. Anything at all that the devil says is a lie.

Every problem has a solution. I pray that the Lord will help you to locate the unprotected forehead of your Goliath, in the name of Jesus.

Prayer: I bring down my Goliath with the stone of fire, in the name of Jesus.

Many problems men are facing today are as a result of the debts owed by their grand parents. Many problems have their history dated back to the days of the ancestors. Historical links are like rivers flowing from a source. If the source of a river is polluted, the whole body is polluted in every direction and length its flows. And if the source of the river is good, the body is automatically good. Good or bad things can be introduced into somebody through the source or the ancestors. Elisha healed a river from its source.

2 Kings 2:20: And he said, Bring me a new cruse, and put salt therein. And they bring it to him.

A dark river has an evil, ancestral transmission. It is a river in which troubles and problems originate. The devil's major target is to shift your attention from the kind of river that flows into your life so that he can continue to hide in the dark to afflict you. There are five levels of evil ancestral transmission.

FIVE LEVELS OF ANCESTRAL TRANSMISSION

1. Inherited curses: Some curses have been issued a long time ago against people, who became the vehicle of our arrival in the world. Curses that were not pronounced against you but which are working against your life are inherited. You come under a curse if your parents were cursed. You need to pray and break loose from the power of inherited curses. Jesus cursed the fig tree and He mentioned its fruit as the major area for the manifestation of the curse. The tree withered away.

Mark 11:14: And Jesus answered and said unto

it, No man eat fruit of thee hereafter for ever. And his disciples heard it.

Many people do not know that the load of curses they are carrying does not belong to them. They inherited them. You can reject and refuse what does not belong to you because inherited curses are exhibits in your life. You don't have to continue with them for all curses have been broken on the cross of Calvary. Jesus was made a curse and a sacrifice to nullify all curses against us.

2 Cor. 8:9: For ye know the grace of our Lord Jesus Christ, that, though he was rich, yet for your sakes he became poor, that ye through his poverty might be rich.

2. Inherited evil covenants: Covenants are powerful agreements sealed by a supernatural power. Evil covenants are enforced and monitored by forces of darkness. As long as an evil covenant is not broken, powers of darkness continue to use it as a ladder to reach the lives of future generations of the children whose parents entered into that covenant.

Many parents and grandparents entered into evil covenants for satanic protection, security, blessing, fruits of the womb, bountiful harvest of farm produce, promotion, victory over enemies in battle, etc. Anywhere an evil covenant is found in the line of your history, it has the power to affect you if you don't reject and break it. Covenants are made on behalf of the people who suffer the consequences in their ignorance. Ask more questions about your family background and ancestors. The Lord will give you the knowledge of the things that are wrong in your life.

3. Inherited evil carryover: A carryover is an unfinished assignment. It is a term mostly used in the university to describe the transfer of a course or a failed examination to a future time. Although the student has left that level, he still has some thing in his past which he has to face in the future.

Many evil things have been left by our parents and ancestors in the past, and if we don't break the basis of their effects on us, the devil will see them as unfinished business and as a carryover into our own lives.

Prayer: I refuse the carryover of any problem from my parents, in the name of Jesus.

4. Inherited evil burden: A burden is another word for a load. Animals used to carry loads in the olden days were called beasts of burden. Men would pack loads and bind them together on the animals for a long journey or for a trip to the market. You may not know about the problems in your ancestors' lives that became a burden your parents carried. Now the same burden is manifesting in your life. But it is not yours, hence you must reject and throw it down. The Scripture says that it is wrong to carry another person's load.

Galatians 6:5: For every man shall bear his own burden.

Prayer: I shatter every load I inherited from my ancestors, in the name of Jesus.

The load which some families carry is that of sickness. Some are carrying the load of calamities, bad luck, premature death and mysterious problems. They have a record of many people in their family who have carried the evil burden. The programme of God for your life is enough burden for you to carry. Reject every load that is not yours and stop being a beast of burden for loads that were not really yours from the beginning. You can refuse and reject them in the name of Jesus.

5. Inherited evil yokes: These are another kind of ancestral transmission. Some children carry the yokes which their parents carried. They continue from where their parents stopped. A yoke is not like a burden. A burden is carried alone or individually, as two people will not carry the same load at the same time. But a yoke is a bond or a link that binds two people together. The direction of one party affects the other. Both of them have to move together in the same direction.

Many of our parents entered into yokes with satan and demons. They went in the direction that the powers of darkness wanted them to go. And because the yokes were not broken, their children unavoidably enter into them. They find their lives going in directions that are against their dreams. What happens is that the devil is in charge of the direction you go, except you break off every inherited evil yoke in your life.

These five levels of ancestral transmission can hinder the fulfilment of your destiny if they are not dealt with. Ignorance in this area can be very expensive. If you don't know what is happening to you, the devil will continue to punish you. But if you can identify and locate them one after another and address them in aggressive prayers, you will be able to move forward.

Abraham was the first man known as the friend of God. He is the first man to be called the father of faith. God gave him specific instructions that had to do directly with his background and ancestral descent. Read the account.

Genesis 12:1-4: Now the LORD had said unto Abram, Get thee out of thy country, and from thy kindred, and from thy father's house, unto a land that I will shew thee: And I will make of thee a great nation, and I will bless thee, and make thy

name great; and thou shalt be a blessing: And I will bless them that bless thee, and curse him that curseth thee: and in thee shall all families of the earth be blessed. So Abram departed, as the LORD had spoken unto him; and Lot went with him: and Abram was seventy and five years old when he departed out of Haran. God told Abraham to get away from three things. One, from his country. Two, from his kindred, that is, his people. Three, his father's household.

We can draw lessons from God's strategy of working out Abraham's deliverance. He had three levels of bondage, so he needed three levels of deliverance, so that he could inherit seven levels of blessings. There will be no manifestation of God's great power in your personal life without your experience of His great deliverance. God separated Abraham from three levels of bondage before blessings came upon him.

The first level of bondage is Abraham's country. What God did for him at this level is called deliverance from national bondage. Your country can be a bondage against the fulfilment of your destiny. If the yokes of your country are not broken in your life, many things can work against you as a citizen of that country.

Most Nigerians need this kind of deliverance because of the image of Nigerians in the eyes of the world. People in many parts of the world don't think or believe there is any good person in Nigeria. Their impression about us is terrible. Those who have been travelling abroad with the country's international passport can tell of the harassment, injustice and dehumanising treatment they and many other Nigerians go through. You need deliverance from national bondage as a Nigerian if you want good treatment in foreign lands. This level of deliverance will help you to fulfill your destiny.

The second level of bondage from which God delivered Abraham can be called community or territorial bondage. Territorial powers have worked against many destinies as a result of which they cannot be fulfilled. Relocating from the village to the urban area does not save you from their operations.

SPEAKING DESTRUCTION UNTO THE DARK RIVERS (21)

There are powers in charge of your town and there is a prince of darkness in charge of your people.

In some communities, nobody ever became great. Somewhere in their rise to fame, they fell, and that is all about them. In some families, nobody ever became a graduate of an institution of higher learning.

Anybody who tried to achieve this there went through unlimited bombardment of satanic attacks because he would be seen as trying to break the status quo. Daughters from some families, communities, towns and villages never stay in their husbands' homes. They marry and soon move out. Some are programmed to late marriages. Others are sentenced to failure in marriage. If you are from any community in Africa, you need deliverance from the territorial powers and from the princes of darkness which work against your kindred.

The last stage of deliverance God wrought for Abraham is called deliverance from household bondage. Many people think we joke in MFM with our kinds of prayer points. Visitors in our midst wonder why we talk so much about praying aggressively against household enemies, territorial bondage and the rest. We do this because God has laid the precedence in the Scriptures. He dealt directly with Abraham and worked these three levels of deliverance for him.

The cage against some people's destiny is from their household enemies. God was specific about Abraham's father's household, therefore you need deliverance from the bondage and enemies of your father's household for your destiny to be fulfilled. God knew the deliverance were necessary for Abraham to possess the seven levels of blessings, hence He delivered him directly. The opportunity you have today is that you can pray aggressively for God to deliver you from these three levels of bondage.

Prayer: You bondage in my father's household working against my destiny, break, in the name of Jesus.

We all need deliverance from the evil powers that control our nation. We need deliverance from the evil powers that control our kindred. And we need deliverance from the evil flow from our father's household. We need these three levels of deliverance like Abraham, if we want our destiny to be fulfilled.

The major powers controlling Nigeria are wastage, corruption, dishonesty, backwardness, bondage, marine powers, rock spirits, witchcraft and familiar spirits, violence, deception, lust for money, treachery and marriage destruction. You need to be delivered and be set free from the cage of these spirits.

You also need to break away from the demonic powers of your village, people, tribe, and region. You also need to break yourself free from the powers and influences of the spirits behind the place of your birth.

Lagos state, for instance, is under the demonic power of the queen of the coast. You need to release yourself from the bondage of the queen of the coast instead of thinking that running to Lagos from your village would solve your problem. You have just arrived at another territory of the powers of darkness. That is why this prayer point from the book

(24) Dr. D. K. OLUKOYA

of Ezekiel is very crucial.

Prayer: This city shall not be my cauldron. I will not be meat in the pots, in the name of Jesus.

Specifically the powers in charge of Lagos state include marine, war, slavery, masquerade and vagabond spirits. If you are from Kaduna state in Nigeria, you .also have to pray very hard. Kaduna means crocodile. The crocodile spirit is in control of the state. There are places in southwestern Nigeria where the spirits of wickedness and poverty are deeply rooted. If you are from Benin, you need to pray very hard against the bondage of idolatry, witchcraft, anger and evil cauldron.

Ilorin, the capital of Kwara state, is like a gateway city. Good things are carried through it but do not have to stay, in the city. If you are from a city like this, you need deliverance from the powers behind this.

Many people do not know that most of the names of our states have to do with water, the marine world. You need deliverance from the powers in charge of these places. If you are from IIaje, a riverine part of Ondo state, IIesha in Osun state or Delta and Rivers states, you need to deliver yourself from the cauldron of marriage destruction. There are many more places from whose powers you have to deliver yourself.

I say this with due apology: Ibadan, the Oyo State capital, is a very large city. It is the third largest city in Africa after Cairo in Egypt and Johannesburg in South Africa. It was privileged to have the first television station, the first football stadium and the first university in the country. The trouble with Ibadan is that it shines for a while and later takes a back seat. As soon as other cities follow its lead, it is replaced and it goes behind them. When the Bible says you should break loose from your kindred, it refers to the powers of darkness in your locality. If you are from Ogun State, you need to pray because Ogun could mean an idol, war, river or charm.

The most serious level of deliverance is to set yourself free from the bondage of your father's household. You need to break yourself away from the satanic flow from your ancestors and parents.

ABRAHAM'S SEVENFOLD BLESSINGS

After receiving three levels of deliverance from his three levels of bondage, Abraham walked into a sevenfold blessing.

Genesis 12:2-3: And I will make of thee a great nation, and I will bless thee, and make thy name great; and thou shalt be a blessing: And I will bless them that bless thee, and curse him that curseth thee: and in thee shall all families of the earth be blessed.

1. Great nation: Abraham was just an individual, but God promised to increase him so much that he would become a great nation. The first blessing he enjoyed was unlimited increase, which turned one man into a great nation.

2. Unlimited blessings: God said He would bless Abraham. When the blessings of God come upon a man, there will never be lack anymore.

3. Great name: Abraham's name is known all over the world because God made his name great. A great name does not die. A great name is not limited to any country.

4. A blessing: You could be blessed with an amount of blessing just enough for you and your household. It is still a limited blessing. But when you are blessed and you turn out to be a blessing to others, then you have entered the level of great blessing. This is the third level of breakthrough Abraham enjoyed.

5. Divine reward: God promised to be Abraham's reward. Anybody that blessed him would automatically be qualified for the blessings of God. Abraham did not have to bother about blessing anybody. God was fully in charge.

6. Divine defence: God made Himself the defense of Abraham. Those who cursed him were in trouble. One, the curse would not work against him. Two, it would return to the sender. And three, God would pronounce an additional curse on those who curse him.

7. All encompassing blessings: God told Abraham

that the seventh level of his blessings is that all the families of the earth would be blessed in him. Jesus was a seed of Abraham, in Him all nations of the world became privileged to enter into God's covenants and blessings.

Abraham would have wasted away as a nobody if he had not gone through the deliverance that ushered him into the blessings. We need his kind of experience to enter into the fullness of God's blessings for our lives. Abraham would have experienced the opposite of what God told him if he had not been delivered in those three dimensional levels. God might have revealed great things to you about yourself and your ministry but except you are delivered from the three-fold bondages, those revelations may never be fulfilled.

Abraham made some unfortunate mistakes after receiving his deliverance. He took some attachments with him as he set out to walk with God. Every evil attachment you carry along with you in your walk with God will slow down your life.

Genesis 12:4: So Abram departed, as the LORD had spoken unto him; and Lot went with him: and Abram was seventy and five years old when he departed out of Haran.

Lot was Abraham's attachment and he became a problem to his destiny later on.

Genesis 13: 10-18: And Lot lifted up his eyes, and beheld all the plain of Jordan, that it was well watered every where, before the LORD destroyed Sodom and Gomorrah, even as the garden of the LORD, like the land of Egypt, as thou comest unto Zoar. Then Lot chose him all the plain of Jordan; and Lot journeyed east and they separated themselves the one from the other. Abram dwelled in the land of Canaan, and Lot dwelled in the cities of the plain, and pitched his tent toward Sodom. But the men of Sodom were wicked and sinners before the LORD exceedingly. And the LORD said unto Abram, after that Lot was separated from him, Lift up now thine eyes, and look from the place where thou art northward, and southward, and eastward, and westward: For all the land which thou seest, to thee will I give it, and to thy seed for ever. And I will make thy seed as the dust of the earth: so that if a man can number the dust of the earth, then shall thy seed also be numbered. Arise, walk through the land in the length of it and in the breadth of it; for I will give it unto thee. Then Abram removed his tent, and came and dwelt in the plain of Mamre, which is in Hebron, and built there an altar unto the LORD.

God revisited Abraham after Lot separated from him. As long as we continue carrying our Lots with us, God will not speak any further about the fulfilment of our destiny. As an attachment in your life, your Lot will blindfold you and make you to disobey God. It is this which slows down one's steps with God. Evil attachments will destroy your destiny and abort the prophetic agenda of God for your life. You should let the spirit of God guard you against every Lot in your life, so that you can move forward.

Abraham again picked up another attachment after the Lord delivered him from Lot. He took Hagar, his handmaid from Egypt, and she delayed the promises and purposes of God concerning his life.

Acts 7:1-4: Then said the high priest, Are these things so? And he said, Men, brethren, and fathers, hearken; The God of glory appeared unto our father Abraham, when he was in Mesopotamia, before he dwelt in Charran, And said unto him, Get thee out of thy country, and from thy kindred, and come into the land which I shall shew thee. Then came he out of the land of the Chaldaeans, and dwelt in Charran: and from thence, when his father was dead, he removed him into this land, wherein ye now dwell.

The accounts in Acts of the Apostles reveal that Abraham obeyed God partially when he took his father with him. He only moved forward with God after the death of Terah, his father.

You have to pray decisively against every attachment in your life. Jabez knew his foundation was terrible and cried out to God desperately.

Ezekiel 16:1-4: Again the word of the LORD

came unto me, saying, Son of man, cause Jerusalem to know her abominations, And say, Thus saith the Lord GOD unto Jerusalem; Thy birth and thy nativity is of the land of Canaan; thy father was an Amorite, and thy mother an Hittite. And as for thy nativity, in the day thou wast born thy navel was not cut, neither wast thou washed in water to supple thee; thou wast not salted at all, nor swaddled at all.

The navel cord of Jerusalem was not cut and so abominations gained free entrance into it. God has a programme for your life, but if you don't cut off the evil attachment in your life, it will not be executed.

JUDAH

Judah was one of the men in the Bible whose dark river affected his background and his generations.

Genesis 49:8-10: Judah, thou art he whom thy brethren shall praise: thy hand shall be in the neck of thine enemies; thy father's children shall bow down before thee. Judah is a lion's whelp:

from the prey, my son, thou art gone up: he stooped down, he couched as a lion, and as an old lion; who shall rouse him up? The sceptre shall not depart from Judah, nor a lawgiver from between his feet, until Shiloh come; and unto him shall the gathering of the people be.

Judah had a wonderful and prophetic destiny. From his tribe, Jesus, the Lion of the tribe of Judah, came to the world. You can see how important Judah was in the programme of God. But he went and married the wrong woman, because the enemy wanted to frustrate God's programme for his life. (Read Genesis 38). Judah went out of his way, gambled with his destiny and slept unknowingly with his daughter-in-law. This flow of immorality into his life nearly cut off his destiny. The immorality of Judah became the foundation of that tribe.

David was a king after God's own heart, but he got the evil flow of immorality from the foundation of Judah, his ancestor. Despite having many wives, he went and slept with Bathsheba, the wife of Uriah, one of his soldiers. This sin cost David joy and harmony in his family. Reprisal killings began as God set His sword in that house.

The same evil river flowed into the life of Absalom who publicly committed immorality with his father's wives. Solomon got the flow of the evil river of immorality to become the man with the highest number of wives in history. To separate Jesus Christ, a righteous seed, from the pollution of His lineage, Joseph was not permitted to sleep with Mary, the mother of Jesus.

Abraham told a lie about his wife, Sarah. Isaac repeated the same lie. Jacob was born and he became a supplanter and told lies. Jacob's wives and children also told lies. The evil flow from their foundation went on polluting them.

LEVI

Levi was the great ancestor of Moses. He had destructive anger in his life which became an evil foundation in that lineage.

Genesis 49:5-7: Simeon and Levi are brethren;

SPEAKING DESTRUCTION UNTO THE DARK RIVERS (35)

instruments of cruelty are in their habitations. O my soul, come not thou into their secret; unto their assembly, mine honour, be not thou united: for in their anger they slew a man, and in their self-will they digged down a wall. Cursed be their anger, for it was fierce; and their wrath, for it was cruel: I will divide them in Jacob, and scatter them in Israel.

The fierce anger of Levi and his cruel wrath eventually flowed down into the life of Moses who in anger, killed an Egyptian. In anger he destroyed the tablets of stone which he laboured 40 days and nights to receive from God. The same anger made him to smite the rock instead of speaking to it as God instructed him. For this reason, he was denied the opportunity of entering the Promised Land. The evil flow from his foundation caught up with his destiny.

Psalm 106:32-33: They angered him also at the waters of strife, so that it went ill with Moses for their sakes: Because they provoked his spirit, so that he spake unadvisedly with his lips.

You need to pray really hard if you are from a polygamous family. You need to stand against every ancestral witchcraft. Abraham was a friend of God, but the river he created flowed down into the lives of his children many generations after him. Judah had a wonderful destiny, but the river of his immorality polluted his generations after him. Moses was favoured to stand face to face with God, but the pollution of anger in his lineage removed him from the privileged position God put him.

The first step you have to take in order to be free is to surrender your life to Jesus if you haven't done so, repenting of every known sin and waging war against every dark river flowing into your life from your ancestors. You must recover your destiny from the hands of the enemy.

CHAPTER TWO

KILLING THE SEED OF GOLIATH IN YOUR LIFE

Prayer point: Point your finger to the heavens and declare: Let heaven open to me by fire, in the name of Jesus.

This chapter you are reading centres on strategic spiritual warfare. This is not another topic. It is a clue that is meant to introduce you to the format it is going to take. As you read on, you will have to pause periodically to take the given prayer points.

If you are a good reader of the Bible, you must have discovered that some foundations were laid in the Old Testament. The New Testament is the manifestation of the Old Testament. The Bible describes the relationship between the Old and the New Testaments in various ways. For example, the Old Testament is called the shadow of what is to come in the New Testament.

Heb 10: 1: For the law having a shadow of good things to come, and not the very image of the things, can never with those sacrifices which they offered year by year continually make the comers thereunto perfect.

The New Testament is the real substance of the Old Testament. The principles and strategies of warfare in the Old Testament are applicable in the New Testament. You need to study and understand them in detail to be able to prevail against the terrible powers of darkness.

Lack of understanding of the Old Testament principles has made many Christian soldiers unfit for the warfare they are called into. The ancient kingdom of Babylon is no more, but the spirit of Babylon is still here in the world. The kingdom of Egypt as it is known in the Bible is no longer with us, but the spirit of Egypt is still working among men.

By the same rule, Goliath, the champion of the Philistines, was killed by David thousands of years ago, but the spirit of Goliath is still in the world today. Therefore, you have to know how to fight spiritually, and how to eliminate the seed of Goliath in your life. For you to understand the reality of what I have just said, the Bible, in the book of Revelation describes a woman in the Thyatira church as Jezebel, which means that the spirit and power behind

Jezebel, the wife of Ahab, were also behind her.

Revelation 2:18-20: And unto the angel of the church in Thyatira write; These things saith the Son of God, who hath his eyes like unto a flame of fire, and his feet are like fine brass; I know thy works, and charity, and service, and faith, and thy patience, and thy works; and the last to be more than the first. Notwithstanding I have a few things against thee, because thou sufferest that woman Jezebel, which calleth herself a prophetess, to teach and to seduce my servants to commit fornication, and to eat things sacrificed unto idols.

The story of Jezebel, the wife of Ahab, can be found in the book of First Kings. In chapter 18, a total of 850 prophets of Baal and prophets of the grooves gathered in an open spiritual contest with Elijah, the servant of God. Jezebel, the wife of Ahab, was the major sponsor of idolatry in the land of Israel. In her days, idolatry and immorality were the order of the day because of the powers behind her. For somebody to command the services of 850 false prophets, she must be a false prophetess too.

Hundreds of years spanned the period between when First Kings and the book of Revelation were written. Jezebel had been destroyed in the spiritual revolution led by Jehu and she had been thrown down from a building and dogs had eaten her flesh.

2 Kings 9:30-37: And when Jehu was come to Jezreel, Jezebel heard of it; and she painted her face, and tired her head, and looked out at a window. And as Jehu entered in at the gate, she said, Had Zimri peace, who slew his master? And he lifted up his face to the window, and said, Who is on my side? who? And there looked out to him two or three eunuchs. And he said, Throw her down. So they threw her down: and some of her blood was sprinkled on the wall, and on the horses: and he trode her under foot. And when he was come in, he did eat and drink, and said, Go, see now this cursed woman, and bury her: for she is a king's daughter. And they went to bury her: but they found no more of her than the skull, and the feet, and the palms of her hands. Wherefore they

came again, and told him. And he said, This is the word of the LORD, which he spake by his servant Elijah the Tishbite, saying, In the portion of Jezreel shall dogs eat the flesh of Jezebel: And the carcase of Jezebel shall be as dung upon the face of the field in the portion of Jezreel; so that they shall not say, This is Jezebel.

Another thing about Jezebel was that she ruled the kingdom of Israel because her husband could not take firm decisions on any state matters. Ahab was so dominated by Jezebel that he took counsel from her on private and state matters. She gained so much control of the kingdom that she single-handedly sponsored the ministries of 850 prophets.

Spiritually, she was in charge of the kingdom and administratively, she took decisions for Ahab. Anything she wanted in the kingdom Ahab gave her the room to get it. She even told Ahab that she was the one ruling the kingdom of Israel and that she could get Naboth's vineyard for him.

1 Kings 21:2-7: And Ahab spake unto Naboth,

saying, Give me thy vineyard, that I may have it for a garden of herbs, because it is near unto my house: and I will give thee for it a better vineyard than it; or, if it seem good to thee, I will give thee the worth of it in money. ~nd Naboth said to Ahab, The LORD forbid it me, that I should give the inheritance of my fathers unto thee. And Ahab came into his house heavy and displeased because of the word which Naboth the Jezreelite had spoken to him: for he had said, I will not give thee the inheritance of my fathers. And he laid him down upon his bed, and turned away his face, and would eat no bread. But Jezebel his wife came to him, and said unto him, Why is thy spirit so sad, that thou eatest no bread? And he said unto her, Because I spake unto Naboth the Jezreelite, and said unto him, Give me thy vineyard for money; or else, if it please thee, I will give thee another vineyard for it: and he answered, I will not give thee my vineyard. And Jezebel his wife said unto him, Dost thou now govern the kingdom of Israel? arise, and eat bread, and let thine heart be merry: I will give thee the vineyard of Naboth the Jezreelite.

What the king could not get from one of his subjects, Jezebel was able to wrest from him through evil machinations. She plotted the elimination of Naboth and gave the vineyard to Ahab. This shows the domination of Jezebel over the kingdom of Israel. The office of a king was the highest administrative office in the kingdom and Jezebel kept that office under her command.

Let us go back briefly to the Jezebel that is mentioned in Revelation. You can discover the exact characteristics of the old Jezebel in her counterpart, that of the church in Thyatira. The pastor or the leader of this church also gave way for the powers of Jezebel to operate. The powers that ruined the kingdom of Israel under the leadership of Ahab attacked the church of Thyatira. They possessed and sponsored another Jezebel and the church leadership lost out. Look at the account again.

Revelation 2:20: Notwithstanding I have a few

things against thee, because thou sufferest that woman Jezebel, which calleth herself a prophetess, to teach and to seduce my servants to commit fornication, and to eat things sacrificed unto idols.

God was against the church because the powers behind Jezebel gained entrance into the assembly and quickly brought in idolatry, evil dominion and immorality, just as in the days of Ahab. As Jezebel, the wife of Ahab, had a large followership of people deceived to follow her wicked ways, the Jezebel in Revelation also had converts and followers, whom the Bible referred to as her children.

Revelation 2:23: And I will kill her children with death; and all the churches shall know that I am he which searcheth the reins and hearts: and I will give unto everyone of you according to your works.

We thank God because He has not changed. He has not changed from working deliverance and miracles in the midst of His people. God gave Ahab's wife the opportunity to repent by sending to her, through

Elijah, prophecies of judgment that would come to pass upon her family. Again, God gave her the opportunity to repent when her false prophets publicly failed.

She should have believed, and confessed like the children of Israel that "the Lord, He is God", but she never turned from her pernicious ways. Her prophets too did not repent. Everybody bowed to God when fire fell from above, but Jezebel's false prophets did not. What happened to them? They were all rounded up and killed. God gave the Jezebel in the book of Revelation the chance to repent too, but she and her followers did not and so God judged them as He did in the days of Elijah.

Revelation 2:21-23: And I gave her space to repent of her fornication; and she repented not. Behold, I will cast her into a bed, and them that commit adultery with her into great tribulation, except they repent of their deeds. And I will kill her children with death; and all the churches shall know that I am he which searcheth the reins and hearts: and I will give unto everyone of you

according to your works.

Look at the word "kill" in verse 23. Elijah killed the converts, prophets and followers of Jezebel. He destroyed 850 in one day. Elijah drew the sword of judgment against them and wasted all of them in total destruction. The Jezebel in Revelation was also killed along with her spiritual children. This is the principle of warfare we are talking about. David killed Goliath. You must kill your own Goliath and his seeds.

1 Samuel 7:1: And the men of Kirjath-jearim came, and fetched up the ark of the LORD, and brought it into the house of Abinadab in the hill, and sanctified Eleazar his son to keep the ark of the LORD.

The short introduction we have about the story of Goliath and the army of the philistines sends serious puzzle to the mind. The enemy advanced and took over Shochoh, one of the territories of Judah. The presence of the army of the Philistines on the inherited property of Judah is a challenge to the Christian soldiers of today. If room is given to the devil, he can possess the possessions of the children of God. He can commandeer the blessings of the children of God and make them his own personal property.

Shochoh belonged to Judah, but the Philistines occupied it. Check your life to find out the areas which satan and his demons are occupying. The enemies can occupy a business and cause it to liquidate. Demons can hijack a marriage and dominate its affairs. Your ministry may be your Shochoh which the spiritual Philistines have occupied. If that is the case, your experience in other areas of life, apart from ministry should be enough lesson to awaken you. Quietly and gradually, the Philistine occupied part of the land belonging to Judah. You have to pray with all aggression to dislodge every power occupying any territory of your life.

Shochoh became the military base of the Philistines in the battle against Israel. Another important lesson can be drawn from here. If you allow the powers of darkness to occupy any area of your life, then you would have given them the opportunity to establish a base of core attacks in your life. A business that has been taken over by the powers of darkness will not be the only area of endeavour that the owner will lose. That is why in the life of a person under the attack of demonic powers, a chain reaction of failure and defeat takes place if satanic activities are not checked immediately.

From business failure the marriage can be affected. The devil wants to gain more control over your life and situation for as long as you allow him. Failure in marriage can lead to failure in ministry, in office work and in the career of children. In acute cases of demonic attacks, failure in an area of life had led to death through health failure. The powers of darkness usually start by gaining control and possessing just an area of a person's life. After they have erected a stronghold, they would move on to attack the remaining territory of the person's life. The Bible warns.

Eph 4:27: Neither give place to the devil.

Total victory comes when you totally disallow the devil and his agents from occupying any territory in your life. What demons need is just a small foothold in your life. If you allow them this, they know what to do with it. Spiritual warfare does not tolerate the presence of the enemy in the camp of the Christian soldiers. The powers of darkness do not have any good mission to accomplish in anybody's life. Therefore, you must not allow any of them to have a hold on you. Their little drops of water can accumulate to make a mighty ocean that will sink your ship.

Galatians 5:9: A little leaven leaveneth the whole lump.

"Ephesdammin" means "the place of blood". Let me explain to you the implication of the enemies' advancement. The Philistines occupied a portion of Judah and got ready to battle in the place of blood. If what you are giving up to the devil is not important in your sight, you will be surprised at the enemies' next level of advancement. From Shochoh, the next level the enemies moved to was the coast of blood. The blood is significant in the Bible. It is the life in any living thing. If you allow the devil to dominate your moral life, he will soon go for your entire life. If you allow the powers of darkness to control you into drunkenness, robbery, fraud and other works of the flesh, they will soon drive you to the place of blood where your very life will be required.

Leviticus 17:14:For it is the life of all flesh; the blood of it is for the life thereof: therefore I said unto the children of Israel, Ye shall eat the blood of no manner of flesh: for the life of all flesh is the blood thereof: whosoever eateth it shall be cut off.

KNOW THE DETAILS ABOUT THE ENEMY

The Bible is not a book of fiction. Every word in it was inspired by God. And if God decides to give details about any subject or person, we are bound, by submission to Him, to pay utmost attention to them. Goliath was an enemy of God's people and led the army of the Philistines to battle against them. God did not just stop at mentioning the name of Goliath, He gave details about him.

1 Kings 17:2-7: And the word of the LORD

came unto him, saying, Get thee hence, and turn thee eastward, and hide thyself by the brook Cherith, that is before Jordan. And it shall be, that thou shalt drink of the brook; and I have commanded the ravens to feed thee there. So he went and did according unto the word of the LORD: for he went and dwelt by the brook Cherith, that is before Jordan. And the ravens brought him bread and flesh in the morning, and bread and flesh in the evening; and he drank of the brook. And it came to pass after a while, that the brook dried up, because there had been no rain in the land.

You need information about the enemy to be able to defeat him. The devil himself relies on information about you to successfully wage war against you. The power you derive from the information and the knowledge you have about the enemy are what will help you to prevail against him in battle. That is why the Bible does not just mention satan and demons. It goes on to reveal their origin and give details about their activities, habitations, strength and weaknesses, kingdom, weapons and the way of victory over them. The Bible gives the following details about Goliath of Gath.

1. Height: His height was the first thing the Bible described. In war, height was an advantage in those days. The presence of a huge, imposing figure was enough to kill the confidence of anybody who wanted to fight him. Goliath had a terrifying height. He was six cubits and a span tall. The importance of height in war was underlined by 10 of the 12 spies that went to spy out Canaan. They felt they couldn't take the land because of the height of the men they saw there.

Numbers 13:31-33: But the men that went up with him said, We be not able to go up against the people; for they are stronger than we. And they brought up an evil report of the land which they had searched unto the children of Israel, saying, The land, through which we have gone to search it, is a land that eateth up the inhabitants thereof; and all the people that we saw in it are men of a great stature. And there we saw the giants, the sons of Anak, which come of the giants: and we were in our own sight as grasshoppers, and so we were in their sight.

Height and strength were closely associated in those days. If an enemy had a great stature he was considered a man of strength. The Bible gives the detail of Goliath's height to make you understand that you must know how high the mountain of problem or an enemy facing you is. The height and size of a mountain determine the instrument to use against it.

2. Helmet: The helmet is used to protect the head. God pictures satan as an old serpent whose head Jesus crushed. The head is the most important part of the body because it coordinates the whole body. Goliath protected his head with a helmet of brass. If the head is cut off, the body will drop dead.

Every power of darkness attacking you has a superior head backing it up. If you are dealing with small demons without paying attention to their territorial superior or commander, the head will arrange other demonic soldiers against you. There are powers of darkness, but there is a prince among them. There are demons but there is a strongman whose orders they executes. Goliath covered his head, because the devil does not want you to know certain things about him. If you know the head behind your problems, you don't have to waste time going for the body anymore.

3. Coat: Goliath's coat weighed 5,000 shekels of brass. It was an armour on its own. The coat protected his body from spears and arrows. The head of the demons in an area has a body of demonic spirits at his command. These demons under him also have some kind of powers they operate which they want to protect. Dislodging them requires extreme violence of your spirit.

4. Legs: The champion of the Philistines protected his legs with greaves of brass. If you shoot a tall man in the leg, he will fall down and you can now cut off his head. There are structures that stand like legs from which demonic powers operate. You have to know these and attack them, so that the powers of darkness relying on them for their operations will crash and scatter. In the vision of Daniel, he saw a

great figure that nothing could penetrate. But the hand of judgment from heaven sent a stone upon its legs because they had a mixture of clay and brass. The legs were the weak points of that figure through which it was demolished.

5. Shoulders: Shoulders are a region of great strength and power. Heavy loads are carried on the shoulders. Goliath protected his shoulders to preserve his strength.

6. Spear: No average man could lift the spear Goliath carried. Spear was a common weapon of war, but Goliath had a special one. Christians know that fasting and prayer are common spiritual weapons. Some fast only for a while and give up. Agents of the devil, witches and wizards, stay away from food for many days to carry out wicked assignments. They use the same weapon of fasting. While an average Christian fasts for three days, agents of dark powers fast endlessly to cause destructions. So, Goliath's spear represents a common weapon fashioned and used commonly by the enemy.

7. Orderly: The last thing the Bible says about Goliath is that he had an orderly who carried his shield before him. The shield was to deflect and quench arrows fired at him. The devil organizes his kingdom in such a way that you have to break through the network of principalities, powers, rulers of darkness and wicked spirits in high places to reach him. Know your enemy before you start fighting.

8. Experience: In addition to the terrifying figure of Goliath, the giant also had the experience of war. From his youth, he fought as a soldier. By the time David faced him in battle, he must have mastered the art of war and how best to use some weapons. The devil and the demons you are facing in battle are well experienced. This is why you have to learn the strategies for spiritual warfare. Don't ever take anything for granted. We thank God that He is Jehovah, the man of war from everlasting to everlasting. Through His strength and anointing, we shall overcome all enemies.

Goliath spoke proudly against the army of Israel. He must have had so much confidence in his armour, stature and experience. He didn't know that Jehovah, the man of war Himself, was the commander-in-chief of the army of Israel. The devil often dares the children of God. He forgets the contest and victory of the cross. A child of God who knows what he is doing will only refer him back to the triumph of the cross.

1 Samuel 17:8-11: And he stood and cried unto the armies of Israel, and said unto them, Why are ye come out to set your battle in array? am not I a Philistine, and ye servants to Saul? choose you a man for you, and let him come down to me. If he be able to fight with me, and to kill me, then will we be your servants: but if I prevail against him, and kill him, then shall ye I?e our servants, and serve us. And the Philistine said, I defy the armies of Israel this day; give me a man, that we may fight together When Saul and all Israel heard those words of the Philistine, they were dismayed, and greatly afraid.

David heard the challenge of Goliath. He offered to take up the challenge and turn away the reproach from Israel. Goliath wanted any man from the armies of Israel to face him. Whoever won would take his opponent's people as prisoners of war. The target of the devil is the man or woman of purpose whom, if he overcomes, gives way for him to enslave more souls. Satan knows the principle of "Smite the shepherd and the sheep shall be scattered". Goliath fell in the battle because the God of Israel fought against him, using David as an instrument.

1 Samuel 17:45-46: **Then said David to the Philistine, Thou comest to me with a sword, and with a spear, and with a shield: but I come to thee in the name of the LORD of hosts, the God of the armies of Israel, whom thou hast defied. This day will the LORD deliver thee into mine hand; and I will smite thee, and take thine head from thee; and I will give the carcases of the host of the Philistines this day unto the fowls of the air, and to the wild beasts of the earth; that all the earth may know that there is a God in Israel.**

There are two words to consider in order to kill the seed of Goliath in your life. The first is "Goliath" and the second is "seed". A sister had a baby and her mother-in-law gave her a waistband to hold the baby to her back, saying that the waist band had been used by all the women in the family. The sister took it and started using it. Suddenly, her tommy began to grow out as if she had another pregnancy.

When she met a man of God for prayer, the first question he asked her was when she would be delivered. As prayers were offered, she heard a snapping sound, then a repulsive odour and water began to flow out from her belly. A lizard came out with the flow and her belly became flat at once. The waistband was used to introduce the seed of Goliath into her life. The prayer against the seed of Goliath shattered the works of darkness in her life. Medical doctors said she had cancer of the liver, not knowing that the seed of Goliath was the cause.

THE SPIRIT OF GOLIATH

The spiritual interpretations of what the spirits of Goliath stand for are applicable to the Christians' present situations. What is the spirit of Goliath?

1. Strongman: The spirit of Goliath is the strongman in charge of your case. A sister was afflicted by a spiritual husband who was the strongman in her life. On her wedding day in the church she was asked the normal questions that precede the union between the bride and the bridegroom: "Will you take this man as your husband..." the minister asked. Her answer was express and frank "No!". The husband cried and pleaded with her to say yes. Nobody knew that the spiritual husband was threatening her, that if she said yes, she would die.

2. Boastful powers: The spirit of Goliath is the boastful power that threatens you. In its manifestation, it may declare that in a given number of days an accident will happen to you or that you will die. Those who threaten that an evil will befall a person in a stipulated number of days are operating under the control of the spirit of Goliath.

3. Confident attackers: Some enemies launch attacks confidently. As Goliath was confident and

presumptuous, these powers and enemies are confident that they will overcome when they attack you. Their confidence is in their strength.

4. Cursing enemies: Those who lock themselves up for a number of days and issue incantations against somebody are agents of the spirit of Goliath. Goliath cursed David in the name of his gods. Such enemies invoke the powers of darkness to back up their curses against their targets.

5. Fearsome enemies: The spirit of Goliath represents fearsome enemies. Their names, operations, attacks and records send fear into people. There are places that people are afraid to mention witches and wizards. Even some churches are afraid to talk about them. This is because of the operation of the spirit of Goliath.

6. Threatening enemies: You must have heard threats like "You are sacked", "I terminate your appointment", "you will never succeed", etc. The spirit that threatens is the spirit of Goliath.

7. Loud enemies: Through the loud voices of some

spirits in their agents, you can recognise the spirit of Goliath in action.

8. Fully armed enemies: Goliath was fully armed from his head to his feet. You need appropriate weapons to overcome the fully-armed enemies.

9. Enemies backed by local idols: Goliath invoked the powers of the idols of the Philistines against David. The spirit of Goliath represents enemies backed by local idols.

10. Enemies that ridicule: The spirit of Goliath is the power that blocks prayers and ridicules the children of God.

11. Mockers: The enemies that mock your God are empowered by the spirit of Goliath. Goliath mocked David and his God.

12. Armoured enemies: The appearance of Goliath represents highly armoured enemies. These enemies are so equipped that it would look as if to overcome them was impossible.

13. Enemies that enforce: In the dream, some people are forced to eat, drink or do things contrary

to their will. It is the spirit of Goliath.

14. Provocative enemies: These are other manifestations of the spirit of Goliath.

15. War-like enemies: If you often see soldiers and war scenes in your dreams, the spirit of Goliath is against you.

16. Intimidating enemies: The spirit of Goliath represents dark forces that intimidate. People who use charms or fetish calabash, wear cowries on the body, or hang gourds around the neck, are agents that manifest the spirit of Goliath.

17. Large opposition: David's experience, in front of a large number of the Philistines, showed another dimension in the manifestation of the spirit of Goliath. If you are faced with a large opposition, the spirit of Goliath is after you.

18. Constant challenges: Goliath kept challenging Israel twice a day for 40 days. The powers that challenge, attack and pursue you constantly are the spirits of Goliath.

19. Proud and arrogant enemies: Goliath was

proud and arrogant. Enemies that are full of pride and arrogance ar motivated by the spirit of Goliath.

Prayer point: Every seed of Golaith in my life, die, in the name of Jesus.

20. Enemies with terrible satanic credentials: The credentials that qualified Goliath as the champion of the Philistines are frightening. Some enemies are like that. They represent the spirit of Goliath. When a person tells you of the evils he has perpetrated, e.g. that among those that dared him, some have died, some have been made mad, etc., he is possessed with the spirit of Goliath.

21. Problems that dominate everything: Goliath dominated the armies of Israel. He also dominated the battle scene. The spirit of Goliath is the enemy that dominates everything.

22. Supporter of our enemies: The mission of some enemies is to support our enemies. This is what the spirit of Goliath does.

23. The enemies' champion: The spirit of Goliath is the enemies' champion. Goliath was not just a

solider of the Philistine army, he was a champion among them. There are champions like that, ultimate powers that lead other powers in attack against the Christian

THE SEED OF GOLIATH

A seed is the part of a plant from which a new plant grows. The seed contains the life of another mature plant. When it is planted and if grows it becomes a complete plant. The seed of a chicken is the egg.

Your mind should picture a tree whenever you have a problem. A tree has roots, branches, leaves and fruits. Problems are like trees. Dealing with your problems from the root is the only key to permanent victory. Many of us go through partial deliverance by dealing with the branches and leaves of our problems. Many ministers of God don't like to deal with the roots of problems because it is a dirty job that stains the hands.

The seed of Goliath can cleverly enter your life. There are many ways the enemy achieves that. But the Lord is ready to work deliverance anytime, anywhere. In as much as God can deliver suddenly, you have to get yourself ready by taking every prayer point raised in this book. The seed of Goliath can be planted in one's life in the following ways:

1. By personal invitation: You can be responsible for the sowing of the seed of Goliath in your life by the life you are living, the name you adopt, and the places you go to. Evil is contagious. You have to break the hold of idolatrous power on your name, if that name is associated with an idol.

I had some unusual classmates in the junior class of my secondary school who used to sit around me. One day, I noticed that one of them just sat down without looking up and was eating all sorts of things. If he was not eating cake, he was licking sugar or sweet. He did that throughout that day and continued the next day with biscuits. A week after, his mother came to the school to find out if he celebrated his birthday the previous week. We said no. We didn't know that the birthday goodies meant for a class of 30 students were what he ate alone. He later developed diabetes because of the excess of sugar in his system. He is an example of one who personally invited the seed of Goliath into his life.

A man took a prostitute home somewhere in Lagos. The next day, he found a coffin on his bed. He invited the enemy. Ask the Lord to forgive you for any invitation you have personally given the enemy to enter your life.

Prayer points:

1. Every Goliath that I invited into my life, go out now, in the name of Jesus.

2. Every Goliath invited by my parents into my life, die, in the name of Jesus.

2. By sin: Sin is a seed of Goliath. The man by the pool of Bethesda was there for 38 years without knowing that it was sin that kept him there. Jesus healed him and warned him to cease from sin, lest a worse thing should come upon him. You can't play with sin and get away with it. Any thought, action, word and desire contrary to the law of God will invite Goliath into your life. Pray again and ask God to

forgive you any sin that has invited Goliath into your life.

3. By inheritance: You can inherit a problem you don't know about. It could be an importation from your mother's or father's lineage. Inherited problems are seeds of Goliath. When they grow untouched, they become a threat.

4. Uncrucified flesh: The works of the flesh are contrary to the spirit of God. The two work against each other. If you cooperate with your uncrucified flesh against the Lord, you are opening the door for a Goliath to come in.

5. Household wickedness: There is hardly a family, especially in African countries, that does not have the problem of household wickedness. It is another manifestation of the spirit of Goliath that troubles the destiny of man.

6. Curses and covenants: Curses and covenants can bring the seed of Goliath into your life. You have to break every curse and renounce every covenant against your life.

7. Witchcraft powers: The operation of witchcraft powers can introduce Goliath into your life. The Old Testament's injunction which says, "suffer not the witch to live", is still relevant in the new covenant, especially in spiritual warfare.

8. Carelessness: Just as anything could enter an open door, carelessness can bring the seed of Goliath into your life.

9. Evil environment: The problems in some people's lives came from the evil environment they once lived in or are living in now. Evil environment can bring the seed of Goliath into your life.

10. Satanic human agents: Human agents of the devil can work evil against us in order to sow the seed of Goliath into our lives

There are overwhelming problems that have the tendency to tie down the soul and weigh down the spirit. If a problem gets to the point of tying you down, it can bring a Goliath into operation in your life.

STRATEGIES FOR KILLING GIANTS

David applied some strategies that brought down the giant. You can apply them to bring down every Goliath in your life.

Know the enemy: David asked, "Who is this uncircumcised Philistine?" He wanted to know about Goliath. You cannot defeat the enemy you know nothing about.

Do not spare anything that can be described as the seed of Goliath in your life.

Take the battle to the gates of the enemy. Your Goliath and his offspring must fall down and die.

Let stones of fire issue from your hands and hit the forehead of Goliath and his children.

Obtain your unchallengable victory today!